# SACRED
## *Self*
# CARE

Elizabeth Griest

Inks and Bindings
888-290-5218
www.inksandbindings.com
orders@inksandbindings.com

# Contents

Dear Reader:

My thoughts/feelings/ponderings/prayers on Sacred Self Care help me.

I Pray they'll help you.

Prayers/Blessings,

Elizabeth Griest

# I

I Believe one's Inner Child holds one's Deepest Feelings/Needs/Wants as well as one's Deepest Beliefs about oneself/others/Life/God.

Further, I Believe one's Inner Child keeps one's memories of this and past lives.

Also, I Believe one's Inner Child carries the Blue Print of one's Sacred Life Plan/Purpose – that which one uniquely can do/live that no one else can.

_____

_____

_____

_____

_____

_____

_____

_____

_____

_____

_____

_____

_____

_____

# II

Through You, Mother/Father God of All my Inner Child and I Realize to Self Care can Never be selfish.

Because You are Not selfish.

And, You, Sacred Parents of All, Guide/Guard Us Always/All Ways.

_____

_____

_____

_____

_____

_____

_____

_____

_____

_____

_____

_____

_____

_____

_____

_____

# III

I Dare to love myself First through You, Divine Parents of All.

---

# IV

Sacred Parents of All, Repeatedly I reassure myself/ my Inner Child I/she cannot be selfish by putting myself/ herself First via You, Divine Parents of All.

I especially remind my Child Self if she/I are meant to temporarily put ourselves on hold/attend to others' needs, Sacred Parents of All Clearly show us. Inwardly and/or outwardly.

_____

_____

_____

_____

_____

_____

_____

_____

_____

_____

_____

_____

_____

_____

# V

Mother/Father God of All, You frequently comfort/encourage my Inner Child/me by causing remembrances of the many occasions she/I stepped back from ourselves while stepping forward to assist others.

Yet, truly/seemingly paradoxically we were still putting ourselves first because we trusted/heeded Your Guidance, Divine Parents of All.

At the Right Time in the Right Way we were able to resume putting ourselves first through You, Mother/Father God of All.

_____

_____

_____

_____

_____

_____

_____

_____

_____

_____

# VI

Please! Sacred Parents of All, Please! Continue to reassure my Inner Child she/I can never be selfish while operating through You.

She has such a Horror of being selfish.

Painful memories of this and past lifetimes, Blame, shame, ridicule, rejection all contributed to my Inner Child falsely believing she was a worthless selfish mistake.

What a false belief! For anyone to hold about her or himself.

_____

_____

_____

_____

_____

_____

_____

_____

_____

_____

# VII

Sacred Parents of All, Guide/Guard me please; plus Guide/Guard everything and everyone in my life.

Thank You, Divine Parents of All.

_____

_____

_____

_____

_____

_____

_____

_____

_____

_____

_____

_____

_____

_____

_____

_____

_____

_____

_____

_____

_____

_____

# VIII

I Want/Need a Balanced Blend of Security and Freedom through Your Divine Protection and Divine Provision for All Your Children, Divine Parents of All.

_____

_____

_____

_____

_____

_____

_____

_____

_____

_____

_____

_____

_____

_____

_____

_____

_____

_____

_____

# IX

Sacred Parents of All, it Comforts/Encourages me
to Wish/Pray for Your Sacred Protection/Sacred
Provision for All Your Children.

_____

_____

_____

_____

_____

_____

_____

_____

_____

_____

_____

_____

_____

_____

_____

_____

_____

_____

_____

# X

Sacred Reminder: I am Divinely Provided for by You, Sacred Parents of All. I am Divinely Protected by You, Sacred Parents of All.

_____

_____

_____

_____

_____

_____

_____

_____

_____

_____

_____

_____

_____

_____

_____

_____

_____

_____

_____

_____

_____

# XI

❖ ·❀·❀· ❖

Sacred Reminder: I am Divinely Guided by You,
Sacred Parents of All. I am Divinely Guarded by
You, Sacred Parents of All.

_____

_____

_____

_____

_____

_____

_____

_____

_____

_____

_____

_____

_____

_____

_____

_____

_____

_____

_____

_____

# XII

Sacred Pondering: I was born because I am Valuable to You, Sacred Parents of All. My life is Valuable to You, Sacred Parents of All.

_____

_____

_____

_____

_____

_____

_____

_____

_____

_____

_____

_____

_____

_____

_____

_____

_____

_____

_____

_____

# XIII

I Believe Self Care through You, Divine Parents of All is Sacred.

Yes, because such Self Care is Honoring You, The Creator Parents, as well as Your Created Child.

_____

_____

_____

_____

_____

_____

_____

_____

_____

_____

_____

_____

_____

_____

_____

_____

_____

_____

_____

# XIV

I Dare to Self Care through You, Sacred Parents of All.

Yes, despite the inner and outer critics.

_____

_____

_____

_____

_____

_____

_____

_____

_____

_____

_____

_____

_____

_____

_____

_____

_____

_____

# XV

I put my Safety and Security First via You, Sacred Parents of All.

For, the Safer and more Secure I am, the Better I am able to give to others, to You, Sacred Parents of All, and to myself.

Even in others' Emergencies when I've had to Solely focus upon their Needs, I endeavor to increase their Safety and Security – as well as mine – by calling upon You, Divine Parents of All.

_____

_____

_____

_____

_____

_____

_____

_____

_____

_____

_____

_____

_____

# XVI

Through You, Sacred Parents of All, I am a Magnet for my Good.

_____

_____

_____

_____

_____

_____

_____

_____

_____

_____

_____

_____

_____

_____

_____

_____

_____

_____

_____

_____

_____

_____

# XVII

Sacred Parents of All, Sometimes when I'm Totally Overwhelmed by Troublesome Personalities and Problems, the Best Self Care I can give myself is to call out to You, Sacred Parents of All, Totally Take Care of me.

Then, some measure of Peace will come to me.

Followed by some Strengthening/Directing Thought and/or action to heed.

Thank You, Divine Parents of All.

_____

_____

_____

_____

_____

_____

_____

_____

_____

_____

_____

_____

_____

# XVIII

Sacred Parents of All, at times my Best Self Care is to Luxuriate in Waves of Comfort and Encouragement You Send me.

Yes, even minus any specific Guidance from You.

_____

_____

_____

_____

_____

_____

_____

_____

_____

_____

_____

_____

_____

_____

_____

_____

_____

_____

_____

_____

# XIX

Healing Self Love Through You, Sacred
Parents of All.

_____

_____

_____

_____

_____

_____

_____

_____

_____

_____

_____

_____

_____

_____

_____

_____

_____

_____

_____

_____

_____

_____

_____

# XX

Healing Self Care Through Sacred Parents of All.

# XXI

Through You, Sacred Parents of All, I love myself NOW despite my imperfections/mistakes/shortcomings.

_____

_____

_____

_____

_____

_____

_____

_____

_____

_____

_____

_____

_____

_____

_____

_____

_____

_____

_____

# XXII

Through You, Sacred Parents of All, I Self Care NOW despite my imperfections/mistakes/shortcomings.

---

# XXIII

I Dedicate myself to Sacred Self Love through You,
Sacred Parents of All.

_____

_____

_____

_____

_____

_____

_____

_____

_____

_____

_____

_____

_____

_____

_____

_____

_____

_____

_____

_____

_____

_____

# XXIV

I Dedicate myself to Sacred Self Care through You,
Sacred Parents of All.

_____

_____

_____

_____

_____

_____

_____

_____

_____

_____

_____

_____

_____

_____

_____

_____

_____

_____

_____

_____

_____

_____

_____

# XXV

I Dedicate myself to Sacred Self Healing through You, Sacred Parents of All.

_____

_____

_____

_____

_____

_____

_____

_____

_____

_____

_____

_____

_____

_____

_____

_____

_____

_____

_____

_____

_____

_____

# XXVI

Through You, Sacred Parents of All, I Devote myself to Sacred Self Love, Sacred Self Care, Sacred Self Healing.

_____

_____

_____

_____

_____

_____

_____

_____

_____

_____

_____

_____

_____

_____

_____

_____

_____

_____

_____

# XXVII

I Give my imperfections/mistakes/shortcomings to You, Sacred Parents of All, for Healing.

_____

_____

_____

_____

_____

_____

_____

_____

_____

_____

_____

_____

_____

_____

_____

_____

_____

_____

_____

_____

_____

# XXVIII

Sacred Parents of All, I allow You to Heal my
Self Doubt, Self Judgment, Self Sabotage,
while simultaneously realizing/growing past my
flaws/errors.

_____

_____

_____

_____

_____

_____

_____

_____

_____

_____

_____

_____

_____

_____

_____

_____

_____

_____

# XXIX

I realize I have flaws, have made mistakes.

I allow You, Sacred Parents of All, to work Healing Improvement in my weaknesses. As well as Healing Peaceful Resolution of my errors.

Thank You, Divine Parents of All.

---
 

---
 

---
 

---
 

---
 

---
 

---
 

---
 

---
 

---
 

---
 

---
 

---
 

---
 

---
 

---
 

---
 

---
 

---

# XXX

Divine Parents of All, Help me Clearly See/
Effectively Employ my Strengths.

# XXXI

Sacred Parents of All, Help me always remember I'm essentially a Contemplative/Communicator/ Companion.

_____

_____

_____

_____

_____

_____

_____

_____

_____

_____

_____

_____

_____

_____

_____

_____

_____

_____

_____

# XXXII

Divine Parents of All, Help me always recall
from my Core of Contemplative/Communicator/
Companion flows my greatest strengths/self care.

---

_____

_____

_____

_____

_____

_____

_____

_____

_____

_____

_____

_____

_____

_____

_____

_____

_____

_____

_____

# XXXIII

Sacred Self Care means, Sacred Parents of All, often taking care of myself in Ways I can't always fathom at first.

_____

_____

_____

_____

_____

_____

_____

_____

_____

_____

_____

_____

_____

_____

_____

_____

_____

_____

_____

_____

_____

_____

# XXXIV

I am allowed to Sacred Self Care first through Sacred Parents of All so that I can help take care of others.

_____

_____

_____

_____

_____

_____

_____

_____

_____

_____

_____

_____

_____

_____

_____

_____

_____

_____

_____

_____

_____

# XXXV

Sacred Parents of All want me to Sacred Self Care first so I can then help take care of others.

_____

_____

_____

_____

_____

_____

_____

_____

_____

_____

_____

_____

_____

_____

_____

_____

_____

_____

_____

_____

_____

# XXXVI

Sacred Self Care can be so difficult for me when I feel overwhelmed by painful emotions, delays, obstacles, hurtful occurrences, hurtful interactions with others.

At such times, I can feel I'll fall apart in a myriad of scattered pieces.

Sacred Parents of All, You understand me.

Hold me close/Comfort me always/All Ways.

Thank you, Divine Parents of All.

_____

_____

_____

_____

_____

_____

_____

_____

_____

_____

_____

_____

# XXXVII

Sacred Parents of All, Provide all my needs Always/
All Ways so I am freely able to Sacredly Self Care.

_____

_____

_____

_____

_____

_____

_____

_____

_____

_____

_____

_____

_____

_____

_____

_____

_____

_____

_____

# XXXVIII

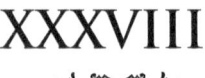

Sacred Parents of All, Provide all my wants that are truly for my Well Being; that genuinely nurture my Sacred Self Care.

Please do so Always/All ways.

Thank You, Divine Parents of All.

_____

_____

_____

_____

_____

_____

_____

_____

_____

_____

_____

_____

_____

_____

_____

_____

# XXXIX

Sacred Self Care is the bedrock of all relationships in my life because Sacred Self Care is founded upon Receiving Your Sacred Care for me, Sacred Parents of All.

_____

_____

_____

_____

_____

_____

_____

_____

_____

_____

_____

_____

_____

_____

_____

_____

_____

_____

_____

_____

# XL

Your Sacred Care for All Your Children is rooted in Universal, yet also Individualized Sacred Care, Sacred Parents of All.

---
---
---
---
---
---
---
---
---
---
---
---
---
---
---
---
---
---
---
---
---
---

# XLI

I Believe Your Universal, plus Individualized Sacred Care for all your children is Your Tree of Life, Sacred Parents of All.

_____

_____

_____

_____

_____

_____

_____

_____

_____

_____

_____

_____

_____

_____

_____

_____

_____

_____

_____

_____

# XLII

Important Reminder: Sacred Self Care often entails following my intuitive Leads.

---
---
---
---
---
---
---
---
---
---
---
---
---
---
---
---
---
---
---
---
---
---
---
---

# XLIII

Valuable Reminder: Sacred Self Care often means thanking You, Sacred Parents of All for providing intuitive Leads.

---

# XLIV

Crucial Reminder: I was given Life for a Purpose. To live as an Individualized expression of You, Sacred Parents of All.

To utilize the Gifts You Gave me to benefit myself, and others You Direct me to.

I Believe such to be True for All Your Children, Divine Parents of All.

_____

_____

_____

_____

_____

_____

_____

_____

_____

_____

_____

_____

_____

_____

# XLV

Another Sacred Reminder: Your Sacred Timing is crucial in so many areas of my life, especially important ones, Sacred Parents of All.

_____

_____

_____

_____

_____

_____

_____

_____

_____

_____

_____

_____

_____

_____

_____

_____

_____

_____

_____

_____

_____

# XLVI

Sacred Parents of All, help me recall Your Sacred Order is crucial in many areas of my life, particularly significant ones.

_____

_____

_____

_____

_____

_____

_____

_____

_____

_____

_____

_____

_____

_____

_____

_____

_____

_____

_____

_____

# XLVII

Divine Parents of All, help me be grateful for Your Divine Timing, Divine Order. Yes, no matter how difficult it is to do so.

_____

_____

_____

_____

_____

_____

_____

_____

_____

_____

_____

_____

_____

_____

_____

_____

_____

_____

_____

_____

# XLVIII

Sacred Parents of All, whenever core centered loneliness takes over, please! Hold me close/ repeatedly reassure me You are with me Always/All Ways.

Thank You, Divine Parents of All.

_____

_____

_____

_____

_____

_____

_____

_____

_____

_____

_____

_____

_____

_____

_____

_____

_____

# XLIX

Divine Parents of All, when I'm engulfed in loneliness! Please! Bring one of Your kind children to commune/communicate/companion with me.

Thank You, Sacred Parents of All.

_____

_____

_____

_____

_____

_____

_____

_____

_____

_____

_____

_____

_____

_____

_____

_____

_____

_____

_____

_____

# L

Sacred Parents of All, Help me be kind to Your lonely Children.

Help me kindly commune/communicate/companion with them.

Thank You, Divine Parents of All.

_____

_____

_____

_____

_____

_____

_____

_____

_____

_____

_____

_____

_____

_____

_____

_____

_____

_____

# LI

---

Sacred Parents of All, Shower me with Your Universal Love for All Your Children.

Thank You, Sacred Parents of All.

---

# LII

Divine Parents of All, Shower me with Your Individualized Love for me.

Thank You, Divine Parents of All.

_____
_____
_____
_____
_____
_____
_____
_____
_____
_____
_____
_____
_____
_____
_____
_____
_____
_____
_____
_____
_____

# LIII

Sacred Parents of All, Help me remember Your
Universal Love for all Your Children is part of the
Root of my Sacred Self Care.

_____

_____

_____

_____

_____

_____

_____

_____

_____

_____

_____

_____

_____

_____

_____

_____

_____

_____

_____

# LIV

Sacred Parents of All, Help me remember Your Individualized Love for me is part of the Root of my Sacred Self Care.

_____
_____
_____
_____
_____
_____
_____
_____
_____
_____
_____
_____
_____
_____
_____
_____
_____
_____
_____
_____
_____
_____

# LV

Sacred Parents of All, Help me remember the Union of Your Universal Love for all Your Children plus Your Individualized Love for me is the Root of my Sacred Self Care.

_____

_____

_____

_____

_____

_____

_____

_____

_____

_____

_____

_____

_____

_____

_____

_____

_____

_____

_____